GREAT CARS
OF THE
FIFTIES

Special thanks to the following owners for allowing us to photograph their cars for these pages: Dan Adams (1951 Mercury coupe), James Adams (1951 Mercury Sport Sedan), Philip Arneson (1950 Oldsmobile 88 club coupe), Bill Barbee (1955 Hudson Rambler), Carl Bilter (1957 Chrysler New Yorker), Bill Bodnarchuk (1957 Chevrolet Bel Air), Pete Bogard (red 1957 Chevrolet Corvette), Joseph E. Bortz (1953 Buick Skylark, turquoise 1957 Chevrolet Corvette, 1957 Pontiac Bonneville), R. G. Brelsford (1950 Oldsmobile 88 Holiday hardtop), Jim Cahill (1955 Chevrolet Bel Air convertible), Richard Carpenter (1955 Chrysler 300B, 1957 Plymouth Fury), Palmer Carson (1959 Buick Electra 225), Kathy Crasweller (1954 Hudson Italia), John Cox (1958 Chevrolet Impala Sport Coupe), Fred Davidson (1959 Ford Thunderbird convertible), Wayne Essary (1958 Chevrolet Impala convertible), Everett Faulkner (1959 Ford Thunderbird hardtop coupe), William Fink (1950 Ford Crestliner), Gary Gettleman (1953 Cadillac Eldorado), Harold Gibson (1955 Packard), Ralph R. Leid (1959 Oldsmobile 98), Bob Patrick (1957 Studebaker Golden Hawk), Chet Pollock (1955 Ford Crown Victoria), Herb Rothman (1959 Ford Thunderbird convertible), Arthur J. Sabin (1951 Kaiser), Neil Vedder (1957 Dodge), Bob Ward (1951 Mercury convertible), Ron Welch (1955 Chevrolet Two-Ten Delray), Alan M. Wendland & Associates (1956 Ford Thunderbird).

Photography
Terry Boyce
David Gooley & Associates
Bud Juneau
Vince Manocchi
Douglas J. Mitchel
Phillips Camera Company

Louis Weber, President
Publications International, Ltd.
3841 West Oakton Street
Skokie, Illinois 60076

Permission is never granted for commercial purposes.

ISBN: 0-517-47931-1

This edition published by:
Beekman House
Distributed by Crown Publishers, Inc.
One Park Avenue
New York, New York 10016

Manufactured in the United States of America
10 9 8 7 6 5 4 3 2 1

CONTENTS

1955 Chevrolet Bel Air convertible

1957 Plymouth Fury hardtop coupe

1954 Hudson Italia coupe

1955 Packard Four Hundred hardtop coupe

INTRODUCTION

1951 Mercury convertible

1957 Chevrolet Corvette roadster

1959 Buick Electra 225 convertible

1957 Studebaker Golden Hawk hardtop coupe

1957 Chrysler New Yorker hardtop coupe

For years, American cars of the Fifties were assailed as overstyled and under-developed, needlessly large and thirsty, poorly built, tastelessly gimmicky, and far from safe. But look a little more closely and you find notable exceptions to several or all of these criticisms. In fact, you need look no further than these pages.

The 25 cars profiled here represent the American industry's best efforts in a decade remembered more for fins and flash than solid progress. Yet there was progress, lots of it. Consider the reliable fully automatic transmission, perfected in the Fifties and all but universal today. The short-stroke overhead-valve V-8 also came to the fore in these years, a clear advance for power and fuel efficiency over traditional L-head engines. The best of the breed powered some of the most memorable performance machines ever built, and many of them are recalled here: the original Olds-mobile 88, Chrysler's 300B of 1956, the first and last of the "classic" Chevrolets, the '57 Corvette, and Pontiac's first Bonneville, also from '57. Of course, V-8s aren't as numerous in today's four-cylinder world, but it's significant that Chevy's landmark 265-cid powerplant is still with us, albeit in greatly modified form. Good things do endure.

Other good things remembered from the Fifties were simply premature. Fuel injection—on the aforementioned Bon-neville and '57 Chevrolets—got its pro-duction impetus in this decade. So too did unit construction. Though it wouldn't catch on until much later, its advantages were recognized even for such dissimilar cars as the early-Fifties Rambler and the 1958-59 Ford Thunder-bird. The former was predictive as the first successful postwar compact, the latter as the pioneer of "personal-luxury," two concepts that would sweep the in-dustry in the Sixties. And we shouldn't forget that the Fifties also popularized the all-steel station wagon and the pillarless coupe and sedan, the body styles that would dominate American production for some 25 years. Not sur-prisingly, many of the Fifties greats pictured here are V-8, two-door hardtops.

The Fifties may have produced some of the industy's worst styling excesses, but it also left us several design mile-stones: the 1956–57 Continental Mark II, the two-seat Thunderbird, the second-generation Kaiser, and Studebaker's "Loewy coupes." All are included, the last represented by an interesting descendant, the 1957 Golden Hawk. You'll also find the original Cadillac Eldorado and Hudson's short-lived Italia, recalling the Fifties as the age of "dream cars," some of which you could actually buy.

There's much more to our *Great Cars of the Fifties* lineup, and all are gems. And even if you didn't grow up with them like we did, you're sure to enjoy the ride.

Fully radiused rear wheel openings, chopped windshield, and chrome wire wheels set the original Skylark apart from other '53 Buicks (owner: Joseph E. Bortz).

6

BUICK
SKYLARK
1953

Some of Detroit's most memorable cars of the Fifties came about quite by accident. Take the original Buick Skylark. According to one account, Buick chief stylist Ned Nickles was busy one day doodling ideas for customizing his 1951 Roadmaster convertible when his boss, division general manager Ivan Wiles, happened by. Wiles was looking for a special model to crown the marque's golden anniversary 1953 lineup, and when he saw Nickles' more rakish, cut-down version of the big ragtop, he knew he had found it. The result was a glamorous limited edition that has since become the most collectible Buick of the decade.

Though historians disagree on the Skylark's design gestation—some say a full-size prototype was built based on Nickles' sketches while others state the styling went from a ⅜-scale clay model directly to blueprints—the basic concept was never in doubt. All Buicks were modestly face-lifted for '53 with a more prominent vertical-bar grille, smoother rear deck, and vertically stacked bullet taillamps, so the Skylark naturally shared these features. But to give the new model its own personality, Nickles raised and rounded the rear wheel cutouts, chopped the standard convertible windshield by four inches, and nattily notched the beltline so it would match the hopped-up aft quarters. Buick's then-customary front fender portholes were conspicuously absent, but a slimmer, reshaped rendition of the make's trademark chrome sweep-spear decorated the bodysides. The finishing touch was a beaut: genuine Kelsey-Hayes chrome wire wheels mounting 8.00 × 15 wide-white tires.

Priced at a lofty $4596, the Skylark made a handsome showcase for several noteworthy mechanical improvements found throughout the '53 Buick line. The big news was the

Skylark dash was basically the same as that of other '53 Roadmaster models. Full carpeting, leather upholstery, and Selectronic signal-seeking radio were all standard. Though this car lacks it, a non-factory continental kit is seen on many examples (owner: Joseph E. Bortz).

division's first-ever V-8, dubbed "Fireball" because of a combustion chamber shape said to produce an ignited fuel/air mixture resembling a spinning sphere. At 322 cubic inches, this compact, overhead-valve unit featured oversquare bore/stroke dimensions (4.00 × 3.20 inches) with ample room for future enlargement, plus the highest compression ratio in the industry, 8.5:1. Not surprisingly, the Fireball instantly put Buick in

third place in the burgeoning "horsepower race," behind Cadillac and Lincoln. With four-barrel carburetor as fitted to the top-shelf Roadmaster models, including Skylark, output was 188 horsepower. A two-barrel 170-bhp version was standard for the mid-range Super series. (The low-line Special made do with Buick's trusty old straight eight for one more year.) Said *Buick Magazine:* "The Fireball V-8 is not a new development. Buick has been developing a V-8 fully as long as other manufacturers, but refused to put it into production until it was thoroughly tested under actual operating conditions." That was the division's explanation for being four years behind Oldsmobile and Cadillac with an ohv V-8.

But the Fireball justified the wait. In fact, its basic block with interim displacement increases would serve Buick all the way up through 1970. Few engines have stood the test of time so well.

Also new for '53 was Twin Turbine Dynaflow, a refinement of Buick's well-known automatic transmission. Standard for Roadmaster/Skylark and optional on other models, it employed a four-element torque converter and two turbines instead of the previous single turbine and five-element converter. The result was more positive shift action, if still not up to Hydra-Matic standards for response. Other engineering updates included a switch from 6- to 12-volt electrics on V-8 cars, first-time availability of power steering and factory air conditioning from Flint, and a gimmicky new "Selectronic" signal-seeking AM radio with foot-activated control. As the costliest offering in the line, the Skylark predictably had all these goodies as standard, except for the A/C.

And there was more: power brakes, windows, seat, and radio antenna, plus tanned cowhide upholstery in your choice of four colors. As for the rest of it, the Skylark was basically a Roadmaster. And for '53 that still meant a big, softly sprung car on a 121.5-inch-wheelbase chassis with what ad writers called "The Million Dollar Ride." Put another way, this was a car far happier in a straight line than it was on twisting mountain roads.

Even so, the Skylark was touted as a "gentleman's sports car." Trouble was, there weren't many buyers of either sex for the best in Buick's 50th year. Production stopped at 1690 units. Only the Roadmaster wagon sold worse. True, the Skylark was conceived mainly as an image leader and not necessarily a money-maker, but that volume was plainly too low to sustain for long. It returned as one of Buick's all-new 1954 models, but this time it was based on the 122-inch-wheelbase platform of the revived Century series and was far less special than the '53. Some say it was less attractive, too. After only 836 copies, the Skylark was put to rest.

Though Buick would resurrect the Skylark name in later years, it's the '53 that enthusiasts remember best. And when you think about it, that's no accident.

BUICK
ELECTRA 1959

One thing about the '59 Buick: it certainly was different. From its slanted quad headlamps to its huge, canted fins, this was the most flamboyant car ever seen from Flint, a clean break with Buick's styling past. Seldom had a make changed character so dramatically or so abruptly. Compared to the chrome-encrusted '58s, the '59 looked like something from outer space. "Buicks so new even the names had to be new," blared the brochures. And for once the usual advertising hype was right.

Model year 1959 marked the third time in as many years that General Motors completely redesigned its entire corporate lineup, something that would be impossible now, even for GM. The reason for this apparent extravagance has less to do with Detroit's longtime devotion to the annual model change than with GM's desire to lower production costs by reducing the number of unique components among its five car divisions. Accordingly, company officials decided that all makes except Cadillac would use a common bodyshell beginning in 1959. As stylist Clare MacKichan explained to author Pat Chappell: "The idea was to make the outer surfaces different so that nobody would know they [bodyshells] were shared, but the things underneath that cost the major amount of money *would* be shared." The upshot was that, because of the decision's timing, GM was forced to junk all its new 1958 designs after just one year.

This change ushered in a new corporate look, and in Buick's case it was definitely for·the better. The main

The 1959 Buick Electra 225 convertible. Base price: $4192 (owner: Palmer Carson).

Buick styling was quite clean for 1959 and dramatically different. Front fender moldings above rocker panels identified Electra 225s, but all models featured a massive dash with a definite "aircraft" influence. Just 5493 of these convertibles were built (owner: Palmer Carson).

elements were rounded lower body contours, long rear decks, and crisp, thin-section rooflines with glass areas so vastly enlarged that they gave new meaning to the stylist's term "greenhouse." Buick wore this styling better than any other make in the corporate camp with the arguable exception of Pontiac, avoiding the vulgarities of this year's Cadillac and the oddities of the "bat-wing" '59 Chevy. Aside from the Buick name, about the only holdover from '58 was the grille, still composed of bright metal squares, though there were now fewer of them.

To emphasize how new its '59s really were, Buick rearranged and renamed its model lineup. The low-line Special became the LeSabre, riding a 123-inch wheelbase shared with the mid-range Invicta series, which carried the mantle of the previous Century as "the most spirited" Buick. Replacing the old Roadmaster and the garish 1958-only Limited lines were the 126.3-inch-wheelbase Electra and an extended-deck companion named for its overall length, the Electra 225. There was no direct replacement for the old Super.

The '59 Buicks also boasted a lot of new engineering. The old X-member chassis was discarded for a clean-sheet K-type frame with boxed side rails, and brakes acquired finned drums, with aluminum used for the fronts. Yet another rework of the hoary old Dynaflow automatic brought Triple Turbine Drive as an optional alternative to the familiar Twin Turbine unit, and Buick's efficient ohv V-8 grew once more, this time to 401 cubic inches and 325 horsepower as standard Invicta and Electra power. LeSabre used the 364-cid version that had been around since 1957, now rated at 250 bhp.

Being new and different was a definite sales asset in the Fifties, yet for all its many changes the '59 Buick was only a mixed success. Though the division built 42,000 more cars for the model year compared to recession-wracked '58, it slipped from fifth to seventh in the industry production standings. It had been a solid third as recently as 1956, and it has yet to rank that high again.

Today, the '59 Buick is at last getting the enthusiast attention it deserves. And that makes it a great car of the Fifties—at least for those who aren't afraid to be...different.

11

CADILLAC ELDORADO 1953

L ook up "El Dorado" in a standard dictionary and you will find it means "the gilded one" in Spanish. You may also find references to "a city or country of fabulous riches held by 16th century explorers to exist in South America" and, more generally, "a place of fabulous wealth, abundance, or opportunity." But Eldorado (one word) has long been synonymous with something far more tangible

than lost treasure troves and mythical realms. For more than 30 years, this name has graced some of America's most desirable and exclusive luxury cars. In the process, it has become inextricably linked for millions of people with one and only one make: Cadillac.

The car that began the Eldorado legend appeared as one of a trio of limited-edition convertibles issued by General Motors for 1953. Buick's

Skylark and the Oldsmobile Fiesta were the others. Though it was something of a surprise addition to the Cadillac line, the Eldorado was actually prefigured by a 1952 show car based on the normal Series 62 convertible, with a predictive "panoramic" wraparound windshield—one of the earliest applications for this dubious design device—and a semi-flush metal cover

instead of a fabric boot for the top well. The Eldorado retained these features, but GM chief stylist Harley Earl reworked the lid so it fit flush with the body. He also playfully cut a notch in the beltline just aft of the doors, as on the Skylark. With its lower-than-stock windshield and standard chrome wire wheels wearing wide whitewall tires, the Eldorado was the sportiest-looking rig Cadillac had offered since the last LaSalles of 1940.

GM's song-and-dance road show, the Motorama, returned for 1953 after a one-year hiatus, and the Eldorado was one of its star attractions. Along with the Skylark, Fiesta, and a fiberglass-bodied two-seat Chevy called Corvette, it was a ''dream car'' you

could actually drive home. But a towering price and deliberately limited production assured that only the very wealthy—and likely the very influential—ever got the chance.

While $7750 may not seem like much for a new car nowadays, it was all the world in 1953 and that's what the Eldorado cost. This and low volume—a mere 532 units for the model year—suggest that this was more a method for testing ideas than a serious sales effort. Indeed, the Eldorado's main mission seems to have been as an ''image'' car intended to reestablish Cadillac as an industry design leader at a time when production styling had seen no major change in four years. The car was a considerable success in these areas.

For those who could afford one, the Eldorado packed just about every feature in the Cadillac accessories book. The list ran to Dual-Range Hydra-Matic transmission and Saginaw power steering (both new the previous year), plus power windows and seat, signal-seeking radio ($120 extra on other models), an automatic heating system ($119 elsewhere), fog lamps, and leather

With its chopped windshield and dipped beltline, the 1953 Eldorado was the sportiest rig Cadillac had offered in years. Chrome wires and wide whites were among the car's many standards (owner: Gary Gettleman).

upholstery. Cadillac's milestone 331-cubic-inch V-8 had tacked on 30 horsepower for 1952 thanks to substitution of a four-barrel carburetor for the previous two-barrel instrument. Tighter compression for '53 bumped the figure up to 210 bhp for all models. Two notable Eldorado omissions were ''Autronic Eye,'' the division's new automatic headlamp dimmer ($53), and Frigidaire air conditioning, a $620 newcomer to the op-tions slate but restricted to closed body styles only.

The Eldorado became much more like Cadillac's standard convertible beginning with the 1954 edition. It would continue in this vein through 1966, sometimes with its own rear-end sheetmetal, often with more standard horsepower than lesser Caddys, always with that special aura established by the '53. Yet despite help from a companion hardtop for 1956-60, annual volume wouldn't exceed 6000 units until the advent of the equally significant front-drive Eldorado for 1967.

While any pre-1967 Eldo is a highly desirable collector's item today, Caddy fanciers generally agree that the '53 (and the equally rare and unique 1957-60 Eldorado Brougham) is first among equals. It's an elegant and ex-clusive original that's as elusive as King Arthur's mine...or El Dorado.

CHEVROLET BEL AIR 1955

By almost any measure, the 1955 Chevrolet was not just a great car of the Fifties but one of the most significant cars of all time. In one stroke, General Motors' volume make erased forever its image as an "old fogey's" car, introduced a milestone engine that set a new standard of performance value for the industry, and left us with some of the sweetest, cleanest styling in postwar history. Today, the '55 remains as much a phenomenon as it was 30 years ago, a car of timeless appeal and enduring popularity, the first of the "classic Chevys."

There's an old saw in Detroit about the danger of introducing new styling and new engineering at the same time. Fortunately, Chevy ignored that "rule" with its 1955 passenger-car line. GM knew well the sales value of styling, so company design chief Harley Earl put together an all-star team to shape this Chevy. Clare MacKichan, Chuck Stebbins, Bob Veryzer, and Carl Renner worked under Earl's dictum of "go all the way, then back off." While the '55 didn't end up as radical as it appeared in early renderings, it wasn't far off. And it was a knockout: longer, lower, wider, and altogether sleeker, with no ties at all to the stodgy 1953-54 look despite using the same 115-inch wheelbase. Notable highlights were a simple Ferrari-like eggcrate grille, fashionable wrapped windshield, a show car-inspired belt-line dip, graceful rooflines, a tidy tail, and just enough ornamentation to attract the eye without offending it.

Overall, the '55 Chevy was attractively trendy, yet it avoided the excesses that marred so many of its contemporaries.

Underneath this handsome exterior was a completely revised chassis, with tubular construction that made it far lighter than the previous frame yet stronger and more rigid. Up front was a new weight-saving ball-joint suspension. At the rear, Hotchkiss drive and a banjo-type axle replaced the heavy torque-tube drive and Salisbury axle of old, and leaf springs were lengthened a full nine inches. It all added up to greatly improved ride and han-

A handsomely restored and nicely accessorized example of the '55 Chevrolet Bel Air convertible (owner: Jim Cahill).

15

Below and right: This 1955 Bel Air convertible displays the deft two-toning and colorful interior trim that pushed production of Chevy's top-line series to over 773,000 units for the model year. All '55s featured a "twin-cowl" dash design inspired by that of the Corvette (owner: Jim Cahill). Center spread and opposite page: From the mid-range Two-Ten series, the popular Delray club coupe, a fancier version of the basic two-door sedan, priced at $1934 with V-8. Total production of this model was 115,584 (owner: Ron Welch).

dling in a lighter, nimbler package.

But the real excitement was under the hood, where Chevy offered its first production V-8 in 35 years. Largely the work of division chief engineer Edward N. Cole, it had been in the works since 1952, with light weight and high rpm capability as major design objectives. ''We knew a certain bore/stroke relationship was most compact,'' Cole said. ''We knew we'd like a displacement of 265 cubic inches, and that automatically established the bore and stroke [3.75 × 3.00 inches]. And we never changed any of this.'' Among the many innovations were individual rocker arms, splash lubrication (via hollow pushrods), and die-cast, interchangeable heads with a common water inlet from the intake manifold. Weighing a remarkable 40 pounds less than the old 235.5-cid ''Stovebolt Six,'' the new V-8 packed 162 horsepower with three-speed manual gearbox (overdrive was a new option) or 170 bhp with extra-cost Powerglide two-speed automatic. For even more sizzle, a special Power Pack version with dual exhausts and four-barrel carburetor was available, offering 180 bhp. It was this last engine especially that enabled ad writers to fairly describe the '55 Chevy as ''The Hot One.'' The name's been with us ever since.

One thing Chevy didn't change for 1955 was its three-tier lineup of economy-priced One-Ten, value-packed Two-Ten, and top-shelf Bel Air series. Included in the last was a last-minute addition that turned out to be the year's most dramatic offering: the singular Bel Air Nomad. A two-door wagon with thin-pillar ''hardtop'' roof styling inspired by a 1954 Motorama show car, it was beautiful and different but pricey ($2500) and impractical. Nevertheless, the Nomad was typical of the excitement and innovation found throughout the '55 Chevy fleet. Buyers were quick to recognize these qualities, which helped Chevy to record production in a year when almost every make scored their best-ever sales. The 1955 model year total was a smashing 1.7 million units, a high-water mark that wouldn't be surpassed until 1962.

With its fabulous '55s, Chevy removed all doubt as to which make deserved the title ''USA-1.'' It's a tradition that lives on today, and that just about says it all.

17

CHEVROLET BEL AIR 1957

In *The Hot One*, author Pat Chappell summed up the 1957 Chevrolet as "a nice way to end a three-year era of superlative accomplishments in design, engineering, and competition." That's putting it mildly: the '57 Chevy was nothing less than terrific. Today it stands as the most revered of the "classic" mid-Fifties models and remains one of the most widely coveted collector cars ever made.

If the '57 Chevy has become something of a "cult" car over the past 20 years or so, it was not an unqualified success when new. Both Ford and Plymouth fielded all-new and discernibly larger passenger cars for 1957, while Chevy had to make do with a heavy rework of its 115-inch-wheelbase 1955-56 platform. Despite an extensive and expensive face-lift, the Chevy looked unfashionably tall, narrow, and dated next to the jazzy Ford and the ultra-sleek Plymouth, and both rivals offered bigger V-8s. Plymouth could boast the most available horsepower and, according to most contemporary motor noters, the best handling. Adding injury to insult, Ford nipped Chevy in model year

production—by a scant 131 units—for the first time in 35 years.

Yet it was the Chevy that would be the most exalted of this trio among enthusiasts. Why? We can think of at least four reasons. First, it retained the trim proportions its competitors had abandoned (as Chevy would do the following year) to the benefit of maneuverability and performance. Second, Chevy had a big edge in workmanship. This year's Fords and Plymouths were notorious for early rust-out, which explains why they're proportionally scarcer than Chevys today. Third, the '57 Chevy was at least recognizably different from the

"Fuelie" 283 V-8 was most commonly installed on Chevy convertibles and hardtop coupes for '57, like this Bel Air (owner: Bill Bodnarchuk).

Top: Chevy's fuel-injected 283-cid V-8 was offered in 250- and 283-bhp tune for '57. Underhood appearance was very high-tech, but the Ramjet system proved troublesome, was not often ordered, and is thus very rare today. Above: Chevy's second restyle on its 1955 platform gave the '57 line a fresh new look. Front-end themes were chosen to impart more of a Cadillac flavor. Right: Discreet front fender emblems identified "fuelie" V-8's presence (owner: Bill Bodnarchuk).

1955-56 models, and if not the last word in trendiness, it was nevertheless pleasing. Moreover, as designer Carl Renner later observed, "I think it was our objective to make [the '57] look like a 'little Cadillac' ...I think that is one reason why [it] sold so well." Finally, the '57 Chevy was a better car than its immediate predecessors in many ways. The chassis was beefed up to handle the extra weight of the longer, restyled bodies, front suspension was revised, the rear leaf springs were moved further outboard to improve road-holding, 14-inch wheels and tires replaced 15-inchers for a lower stance, and gearing was altered to enhance off-the-line acceleration.

But the big engineering news was a bored-out version of Chevy's already famous small-block V-8 and the first fuel injection system ever offered by a mass-market domestic nameplate. Displacing 283 cubic inches, the new powerplant packed 185 horsepower in base two-barrel trim and 245/270 bhp with four-barrel carburetor. The numbers read 250/283 bhp when you specified "Ramjet" fuel injection, but high price and several sticky service problems held passenger-car installations to a mere 1503 units. Interestingly, the 283-bhp 283 was *not* the first U.S. production engine to achieve the magic "1 bhp per c.i." as Chevy's advertising implied: the 354-cid hemi in the Chrysler 300B had performed that trick the year before. Equally problematic was Turboglide, a complicated three-speed automatic introduced this year as Chevy's answer to Hydra-Matic. It lasted only a few years longer than the "fuelie," at least in the passenger models, being phased out in 1961 for Hydra-Matic itself.

Obviously, the '57s weren't trouble-free, but they were the fastest Chevys yet. Typically, a four-door sedan with automatic and the 270-bhp V-8 could run 0-60 mph in 10 seconds flat and the standing quarter-mile in 17.5 seconds at about 80 mph, more than enough for the opposition.

Alas, 1957 brought the Automobile Manufacturers Association's "anti-racing" edict, which brought a temporary end to hot Chevys that could carry more than two passengers. And that's probably the main reason the '57s are still so fondly remembered. They were the last of a truly special breed.

CHEVROLET
CORVETTE 1957

H ad it not been for Ford's first Thunderbird, we might not have a Chevrolet Corvette today. In early 1955, profit-minded General Motors executives were ready to kill off Chevrolet's fiberglass-bodied two-seater, which had not made much of an impression in the miniscule sports car market since its debut in late 1953. But Dearborn's posh new "personal" car was a challenge that GM's pride would not allow to go unanswered, so the Corvette was granted a last-minute stay of execution.

Car lovers have been grateful ever since, for the reprieve brought a renaissance. The second-generation 1956-57 Corvette was a vast improvement on the awkward 1953-55 original, and it secured the future for what Chevy could at last rightfully claim as "America's Only True Sports Car."

Compared to its slab-sided, "plastic bathtub" predecessor, the '56 Corvette was stunning. GM design director Harley Earl came up with fresh new styling that was tasteful in an age of garishness, yet sexy, low-slung, and

distinctly American. Its only questionable elements were phony air scoops atop the front fenders, dummy knock-off hubs on the wheel covers, and a dash that was more flash than function. If the '56 looked like a more serious sports car, it was also more civilized, with new seats, standard

Corvette styling didn't change for '57—and didn't need to (owner: Joseph E. Bortz).

21

roll-up door glass instead of the previous—and clumsy—snap-in side curtains, and an optional lift-off hardtop providing sedan-like weather protection. The Corvette had grown up.

Underneath this new finery was a chassis heavily reworked by a recently hired, Belgian-born mechanical wizard named Zora Arkus-Duntov. Without upsetting the already near-equal weight distribution, he tightened up both steering response and handling. Though understeer was still a tad excessive and the cast-iron, all-drum brakes "faded into oblivion" in hard stops, the revised chassis was a revelation and the 'Vette was now as quick through turns as it was on the straights.

And quick it was. Chevy's superb 265-cubic-inch V-8, designed largely by division chief engineer Edward N. Cole, had been an option fitted to all but a handful of '55 production models. Now it was standard, packing 210 horsepower in normal tune or 225 bhp with high-compression heads. It was mated to the close-ratio three-speed manual gearbox introduced late in the '55 model run, while the formerly standard Powerglide automatic shifted to the options column. In its most potent form, the '56 could hit 60 mph from rest in 7.5 seconds and top 120 mph.

There was no need to change the Corvette's handsome styling for '57, but Chevy upped the performance ante in a big way. The revvy small-block was bored out for 283 cid and offered in five versions ranging from 220 bhp to an amazing 283 bhp, the latter courtesy of "Ramjet" fuel injection. In May, a four-speed Borg-Warner manual transmission arrived as a $188 option, and combined with available axle ratios as short as 4.11:1 to make the "fuelie" '57 thunderingly fast. Tests showed 0-60 mph in 5.7 seconds, 0-100 mph in 16.8, the standing quarter-mile in 14.3 seconds at 96 mph, and a 132-mph max velocity.

Corvette production rose from 1955's low of 674 units to 3467 for '56, then to 6339 for '57. Of the last, only 240 got the troublesome fuel injection system, but it left a lasting impression. So did the 1956-57 design. Today, many enthusiasts regard these as the best Corvettes of all, the 1963-67 Sting Ray notwithstanding. One thing's for sure: they were truly great cars of the Fifties.

Below and right: Optional 1956-57 lift-off hardtop came directly from a '54 Motorama show Corvette. The '57 cockpit was snug (owner: Joseph E. Bortz). Below: Smoother rear deck and fenders and elliptical bodyside "coves" marked the second-generation 'Vette. Here, another superb '57 (owner Pete Bogard).

CHEVROLET IMPALA 1958

Mention "Impala" and most people think "Chevrolet." For the better part of 25 years, this name has been virtually synonymous with America's perennial best-selling make as its most popular model line and the nation's favorite family car. In the beginning, however, "Impala" meant something very special.

The Impala debuted as the flagship of a 1958 Chevrolet fleet virtually all-new from the ground up. Conceived as a "Bel Air Executive Coupe," it was intended to take Chevy out of the low-price field and into the bottom end of the medium segment, which product planners had concluded would be the biggest growth market of the late Fifties.

Predictably, all '58 Chevys emerged bigger and heavier than the agile, spirited 1955-57 models. Enthusiasts have long ignored the '58s, including the Impala, for this reason, but Chevy was only playing catch-up with Ford and Plymouth, both of which had moved away from their "mid-size" 1955-56 platforms the year before.

And in retrospect, the '58 Chevy was a generally much improved car with a lot of what buyers wanted. Its new X-member chassis was not only stronger but yielded a smoother ride, thanks to a 2.5-inch longer wheelbase (117.5 inches) and a new four-link rear suspension with coil instead of leaf

The first Impala Sport Coupe featured a longer rear deck than other '58 Chevy hardtops (owner: John Cox).

springs. The latter was designed to facilitate installation of "Level Air," but the airbag springs were prone to leaks and the option found few takers at $124. Of greater interest was a larger optional V-8, the new 348-cubic-inch "Turbo Thrust" unit offering 250 horsepower, or 280 bhp with 9.5:1 compression and three dual-throat carburetors. In either guise it made any '58 Chevy quite quick—maybe not as fast as a "fuelie" '57 but quick enough to qualify as a "Hot One." The 250-bhp Bel Air hardtop sedan could run 0-60 mph in a respectable 9.9 seconds, and *Motor Trend* timed a 280-bhp Impala coupe at 9.1 seconds, with 16.5 seconds for the standing quarter-mile. Both these figures were achieved with Turboglide, Chevy's three-speed automatic offered as an alternative to two-speed Powerglide at

$231. Veteran tester Tom McCahill said it was "as smooth as velvet underpants" when working properly, something it didn't do very often.

Chevy styling was more Cadillac-like for '57, and the '58 continued the trend. Though it's always been somewhat controversial, it was at least distinctive—and far less glittery than this year's Buick and Oldsmobile. Both Impala convertible (the only one in the Chevy line) and hardtop coupe were set apart from their Bel Air sisters by stainless-steel rocker moldings, special emblems and wheel covers, and dummy "pitchfork" scoops ahead of the rear wheels. Yet contrary to popular opinion, this was more than just fancy trim. The Impala's lower body was completely different from that on other '58s, though overall length was the same, thanks

to a longer rear deck. Inside exclusives ran to brushed-aluminum door panel trim, color-keyed horizontally striped upholstery, and a pull-down rear armrest below a central radio speaker grille.

The '58 Impala proved so attractive that it became the new top-line series for 1959. But the concept was watered down, and except for the Super Sports of the Sixties, none of the later Impalas would be as unique as the original. Though it's taken 25 years, enthusiasts have at last rediscovered "The Forgotten Hot One," reason enough to include it here as a great car of the Fifties.

This pristine 1958 Impala convertible looks like something out of Chevy's accessory catalog. It's typical of many first-year Impalas found on the collector market today (owner: Wayne Essary).

26

CHRYSLER 300B 1956

No list of great Fifties cars could be complete—or honest—without at least one Chrysler 300. There are five in this decade, from the original C-300 of 1955 to the 300E of 1959, and all could be included. Each was—and is—a thoroughbred: big, luxurious, superbly engineered, blindingly quick, the ultimate expression of Chrysler performance in its year. But if we had to pick just one, it would have to be the 300B of 1956. It was the last letter-series model the factory would campaign in open competition, and it was arguably the most elegant 300 of the early years. Moreover, it boasted several noteworthy technical improvements. One of them has a timeless spell for anyone enchanted by high-performance iron: an engine that exceeds the magic "one horsepower per cubic inch" ideal.

The B was a direct descendant of the C-300, introduced in February 1955 as a limited-edition capper for Chrysler's dramatically new "Forward Look" corporate lineup. The model designation stemmed from the rated horsepower of its 331.1-cid "FirePower" hemi-head V-8, which made this the most powerful production car in the world. Tom McCahill of *Mechanix Illustrated* called it "a hard-boiled, magnificent piece of semi-competition transportation, built for the connoisseur."

Indeed, a connoisseur was behind it: Chrysler Division chief engineer Robert M. Rodger, who was part of the team that developed the hemi V-8 for 1951. Now he added a special cam, mechanical lifters, and twin four-barrel carbs, and beefed up the chassis with high-rate front coil and rear leaf springs and heavy-duty shock absorbers. Meanwhile, company styling chief Virgil Exner teamed

Except for higher flying rear fenders, the 300B looked much the same as its 1955 C-300 predecessor (owner: Richard Carpenter).

with Cliff Voss and Tom Poirer on a unique styling package for the potent drivetrain, a deft blend of the New Yorker hardtop coupe bodyshell, Windsor rear quarter panels, and Imperial front end and wire wheels. McCahill called the result "as solid as Grant's tomb and 130 times as fast," and reported a 0-90 mph time of 16.9 seconds on the Daytona Beach sands.

Chrysler built 1692 of the 1955-model 300s (plus 32 more and a bare chassis for export), and sold them at around $4000 apiece. Radio, heater, and power steering were the only major options. Air conditioning, backup lamps, and two-tone paint weren't available, but tan leather upholstery was standard. The C-300

quickly began tearing up the race tracks, and by season's end had won 37 NASCAR and AAA races of 100 miles or more. A legend had been born.

Aside from more prominent tailfins, the 1956 follow-up, designated 300B, was unchanged in appearance. Air conditioning was now optional and badly needed 12-volt electrics were adopted. But the big news was a hemi bored out to 354 cid for 340 bhp on standard 9.0:1 compression or 355 bhp with optional 10.0:1 heads. McCahill dubbed it the "mastodon of muscle," while Chrysler quietly called it "America's Most Powerful Car." The 300B cleaned up at the Daytona Speed Weeks. Tim Flock's Kiekhafer Racing car won this year's 160-mile

Grand National event at a 90-plus mph average, and another set an unofficial stock car record in the flying-mile at 142.914 mph. Yet the roadgoing B was a highly civilized car that could be more personalized than the '55. Buyers could now specify three-inch dual exhausts, axle ratios ranging from 3.08 to an ultra-short 6.17:1, plus tinted glass and Chrysler's unique "Highway Hi-Fi," a gimmicky forerunner of today's compact audio disc players. Initially, two-speed PowerFlite automatic with pushbutton control was the only transmission available, but it was superseded at mid-year by three-speed TorqueFlite, one of the finest self-shifters ever created. The 300B

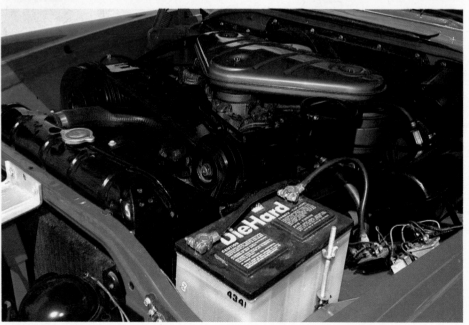

saw fewer copies than the C-300—just 1102. But it didn't matter: every one was sold.

With the all-new 300C of 1957, the letter series began moving away from all-out performance toward high-style personal luxury. Thus, the B stands as the last of the "pure" 300s, and that makes it an undisputed Fifties great.

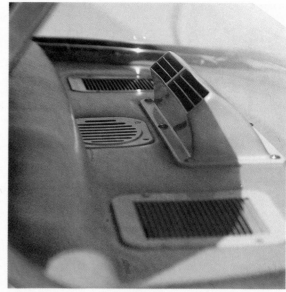

Far right: Factory air conditioning was a new 300 option for '56, identified by small rear fender scoops and a raised vent on the package shelf. Below left: The 1955-56 instrument panel was another Imperial item borrowed for the 300. Speedometer was calibrated to 150 mph. Tan leather upholstery was standard. Bottom left: The 300B's 354-cid hemi V-8 (owner: Richard Carpenter).

CHRYSLER NEW YORKER 1957

Chrysler Corporation underwent a design metamorphosis in the mid-Fifties—and just in time. It was instigated by then-president L. L. Colbert, who had concluded that the firm's falling sales since 1949 were largely due to the dull, boxy styling favored by his predecessor, K. T. Keller. Colbert ordered a corporate-wide restyle for 1955 at a reported tooling cost of $100 million. Developed under newly named design chief Virgil Exner, the "Forward Look" line was a solid hit and sales improved. But Colbert wanted more, so he earmarked $300 million for another top-to-bottom overhaul that would arrive just two years later. The result was as unbelievable as it was unexpected. With its radically changed 1957 models, Chrysler decisively seized industry design leadership from General Motors and, in so doing, forever banished its staid styling image.

Though all the company's '57s looked good, Chrysler was arguably the best of the bunch. From the clean horizontal-bar grille to the gracefully upswept rear fenders, it was the sort of unified design that only could have

A much lower "dart" profile made the '57 New Yorker look longer even though it wasn't. Colorful cabin was typical of the period. Quad lights were newly available where legal (owner: Carl Bilter).

Chrysler was arguably Highland Park's handsomest car for '57, especially the top-line New Yorker. The frontal treatment almost qualifies as a combination bumper/grille, and was tasteful yet appropriately massive. Hardtops featured a higher backlight than other models, but graceful fin/taillight assembly was common to all. The New Yorker's hemi V-8 was enlarged to 392 cubic inches and 325 bhp for '57 (owner: Carl Bilter).

come from one mind, not several. The dart-shaped profile, lower beltline, big new expanses of glass, and striking height reductions (three inches on sedans, five on hardtops) combined to suggest greater overall length, yet the '57s were actually a bit *shorter* than the '56s. In all, this "New Look of Motion" was distinctive and exciting yet commendably restrained for the period. It made the '57 exactly what Chrysler claimed, its "most glamorous car in a generation."

Along with its corporate cousins, the '57 Chrysler introduced two major mechanical innovations. One was "Torsion-Aire Ride," a new front suspension consisting of longitudinal torsion bars acting on lower transverse arms, plus upper A-arms and an anti-roll bar. Despite its name, it was designed mainly for improved handling with no penalty in ride comfort. It made Chrysler Corporation's cars the most roadable in the industry for '57, assisted by new box-rail chassis with wider tracks and lower centers of gravity.

Highland Park's other technical triumph for '57 was TorqueFlite, a new three-speed automatic offered throughout the company stable as an optional alternative to two-speed PowerFlite. Also featuring pushbutton control, it was hailed for its quick response and smooth shift action. It would prove so good that it's still with us in the Eighties.

The 1957 Chrysler line comprised three series, all riding a 126-inch wheelbase as for 1955-56. After a five-year absence, the Saratoga returned as a new mid-price offering, powered by a 354-cubic-inch hemi-head V-8 with 285 horsepower. The base Windsor group used this same powerplant but with 10 fewer horses. Continuing at the top of the heap was the plush New Yorker, which acquired a bored-and-stroked 392-cid hemi rated at 325 bhp. Included in this line was the limited-edition 300C, with 375 or 390 bhp, plus a new honeycomb trapezoidal grille not shared with other models, along with the usual full-house equipment.

Chrysler workmanship took a nose dive for '57. Early rust-out was the main flaw, and it led many of these brilliant cars to an early grave. Of course, that only makes survivors like the one here that much more special. And there's justice in that.

CONTINENTAL
MARK II 1956–57

Great cars are never forgotten, and the original Lincoln Continental is one of them. In the early Fifties, memories of Edsel Ford's timeless 1940-41 design prompted dealers and would-be owners to ask Ford Motor Company for a successor, the first new Continental since the last of the postwar continuations was built in 1948. The result was a great car of the Fifties: the unforgettable Mark II.

Ford decided to answer pleas for a new Continental during its Golden Anniversary year, 1953. After a long period of design stagnation, executive

upheavals, and eroding sales, the firm had made a spectacular recovery on the strength of its all-new 1949 corporate line. The fleet was again completely redesigned for 1952, when Ford regained the industry's number-two rank from a faltering Chrysler Corporation. With profits healthier than at any time since the war, it seemed natural to consider a super-luxury model aimed at establishing Dearborn's dominance at the very top of the market—even above Cadillac.

The Continental project began as a competitive affair between five out-

side consultants and the company's own newly created Special Projects Division headed by William Clay Ford, younger brother of president Henry Ford II. Management looked at 13 different proposals and—to no one's surprise, perhaps—unanimously selected the in-house design.

It was a fine choice: exceptionally clean, dignified without being stuffy, and—most important—thoroughly

The Continental Mark II evoked the classic simplicity of its 1940-41 forebear yet was thoroughly modern.

evocative of 1940-41. Though its long-hood/short-deck proportions weren't as pronounced as on the original, the Mark II did have the same sort of close-coupled cabin. And it maintained tradition with a trunklid styled to resemble a "continental" spare. The understated exterior was matched by an equally low-key interior. Four round dials housed a complete set of working instruments, including a tachometer, in a starkly simple dash, with an embryonic center console carrying aircraft-inspired toggle levers for heating, ventilation, and air conditioning.

Introduced for 1956, the Mark II was virtually handcrafted on a unique "cowbelly" chassis designed by Harley F. Copp. It dipped low between the axles to permit upright

seating without a high roofline. Wheelbase was 126 inches, overall length was 218.5 inches. Power was supplied by Lincoln's 368-cubic-inch V-8, rated at 285 horsepower for '56. Output rose to 300 bhp for '57, when removal of the central frame member brought curb weight down from an initial 4825 pounds to a still-hefty 4797. Engines were specially selected from the assembly line, individually balanced, and teamed with Multi-Drive three-speed automatic transmissions pulling 3.07:1 rear axles.

Though the Mark II earned design plaudits on both sides of the Atlantic, it didn't earn Ford any money. In fact, the firm lost an estimated $1000 on every one it sold despite a truly mind-boggling base price of nearly $10,000. After building just 1325 of the

'56s and 444 of the minimally changed '57s, Ford gave up on the super-luxury concept, ironically just as Cadillac was taking it up with the Eldorado Brougham. For 1958, the Mark II was replaced by a Lincoln-based giant called Mark III. Though it cost less to build and sold far better, it was far less distinctive than the Mark II—and best forgotten.

But the Mark II lives on in our memory. As one Ford official put it: "What we had going for us...was literally a revival of the Duesenberg concept." And that's why it will always be remembered.

A long hood, short deck, and a close-coupled cabin gave the Mark II a slightly sporting air. Humped trunklid has since become a Continental trademark.

DODGE CUSTOM ROYAL LANCER 1957

G litter and go were the unques-
tioned keys to sales success in the
Fifties, and the 1957 Dodge was a
perfect symbol of the age. It was
longer, lower, and wider, chromier
and more colorful, faster and flashier
than anything the division had ever
offered. And appropriately enough, it
was the most popular Dodge of the
decade. Model year production was
nearly 288,000 units, a gain of over
37,000 from 1956, and Dodge moved

from eighth to seventh on the industry volume list.
    Like its Chrysler Corporation
siblings, Dodge was virtually all-new
for '57. The only holdovers were
engines, and even in that area there
were plenty of changes. As with people, not all automotive "children" are
treated equally by their corporate
"parents," and most critics agree that
Dodge got the short end of Highland
Park's styling stick this year. It was

certainly the busiest-looking member
of the family, with a heavy horizontal-
bar grille, prominent "eyebrows"
over the headlamps, wild two-toning,
and "saddle shoulder" fins above
thrusting taillamps that suggested a
jet plane's exhaust ports. Dodge
described all this as "Swept-Wing"
styling, but surely no aircraft was so
contrived.
    Few argued with the dramatically
altered silhouette. Dodge naturally

came in for Chrysler Corporation's new torsion-bar front suspension this year. As with its linemates, this necessitated a completely new and much lower box-rail frame, with a recessed rear floor—shades of the Step-down Hudson—that allowed greatly reduced overall height without a great loss of interior space. Accordingly, stylists lowered sedan and wagon rooflines by three inches and hard-tops by a whopping five. Adoption of 14-inch-diameter wheels and tires (an inch smaller than before) and a two-inch longer wheelbase (up to 122 inches) helped, and the Custom Royal Lancer hardtop you see here measured a mere 56.8 inches from road to roof. Despite the much sleeker appearance, overall length was unchanged at 212.2 inches. Overall width was changed,

however, bulging by 3.3 inches to 77.9. As we said, longer, lower, wider.

Dodge was well-established as Chrysler's performance division by 1957, and its engine lineup this year only solidified that position. The mainstay was still the efficient, fairly low-cost polyspherical-head V-8, which had come to Dodge for 1955 and was stroked from 3.25 to 3.80 inches for '56. Now bore was stretched, from 3.63 to 3.69 inches, to boost displacement from 315 to 325 cubic inches. Higher 8.5:1 compression, larger intake valves, and a new cam-shaft profiled for faster valve opening were also specified. The base two-barrel version put out a rated 245 horsepower and was the standard V-8 for the low-line Coronet and mid-range Royal models. The top-shelf

Custom Royal carried a four-barrel car-buretor, good for 260 bhp. For flat-out flying you ordered the D-500 option, available across the board in any body style, even the plain-Jane two-doors. This year there were two D-500s, a four-pot high-compression (9.25:1) unit with 285 bhp and a twin four-barrel version with 310 bhp. Both were packaged with high-rate front torsion bars and rear leaf springs plus stiffer shocks, and cars so equipped exhibited what *Motor Trend* magazine called "close liaison with the road."

Undoubtedly, the V-8 Dodges were among the industry's hottest cars for '57. They were still fairly light despite

This beautifully restored '57 Dodge Custom Royal Lancer carries the rare D-500 option. It's a recent Walter P. Chrysler Club national meet winner (owner: Neil Vedder).

37

their dimensional changes, and the bigger poly's extra power and torque were more than enough to compensate for the few extra pounds. Even the mild 245-bhp setup could turn 0-60 mph times of less than 10 seconds, and the D-500s were simply astounding off the line. One writer aptly termed the '57 Dodge "the dream with the runaway horses." And run it certainly did.

Of course, automatics were all the rage in 1957, and Dodge gained one of the best in Chrysler's new three-speed TorqueFlite. Quick and positive yet very smooth, it mated beautifully with the more powerful V-8s. It also proved very rugged and trouble-free right out of the box, and even drag racers began favoring it over stick-shift transmissions—not to mention the vast majority of Dodge buyers.

It's difficult to think of a year more successful for Dodge than 1957. And indeed, it would be a long time before the division would again have as much innovation, excitement, and flair in a single season. Though its performance would always be among Detroit's best, progressively more bizarre styling and the substandard workmanship that began with the '57s would hurt Dodge greatly

through the early Sixties.

So 1957 ranks as a watershed year for Dodge, and a large band of marque loyalists recognize it as such today. More than a symbol, the "Swept-Wing" '57 remains a great car of the Fifties.

The Custom Royal Lancer's rear aspect shows clearly why Dodge referred to its '57 styling as "Swept-Wing" design. D-500 option was signaled only by a discreet emblem on the right side of the trunk, plus the dual exhausts. Of course, they were also easy to pick out at stoplights, where they moved away fast. Interior was as jazzy as the exterior (owner: Neil Vedder).

FORD CRESTLINER 1950

Ford Motor Company entered the Fifties breathing a collective sigh of relief. The all-new 1949 Ford had been the big sales success the firm so desperately needed it to be, and Dearborn was on its way to a healthy $177 million profit for the calendar year. There was little need for the encore edition to be changed except in detail, and the '49's tremendous tooling costs left little money anyway. But there was a last-minute addition for 1950, a glamorous new line leader in the Custom V-8 series. Its name was Crestliner.

The Crestliner was Ford's reply to the sporty "hardtop convertible," originated in production by General Motors' senior makes for 1949. The two-door pillarless style had found immediate buyer favor, and Ford knew that arch-rival Chevrolet would get one for 1950. What to do? Why not a spiffy Tudor sedan with the look, if not the actual function, of a hardtop?

George Walker's styling staff went to work. Among its members was Gordon M. Buehrig, famed for his Auburn, Cord, and Duesenberg designs of the mid-Thirties. Buehrig suggested a two-tone paint treatment in the image of the classic "LeBaron sweep" from the custom-body era, so the Crestliner emerged with elliptical chrome bodyside moldings that

delineated a broad area for the contrast color. A matching vinyl roof covering was specified to emphasize the "convertible" aspect. Rear fender skirts, anodized-gold front fender name script, and a posh, color-keyed interior provided the finishing touches.

Priced at $1711, the Crestliner was the costliest model in the 1950 line, $200 above the regular Custom Tudor. Despite that and its late start, this "factory custom" scored a respectable 17,601 model year sales.

The Crestliner benefited from a

The Crestliner bowed for 1950 as Ford's stand-in for a pillarless hardtop. It was available only with V-8 as part of the Custom series (owner: William Fink).

number of detail revisions made to all Fords that year, billed as ''50 Ways New...50 Ways Finer.'' Most were dictated by the rush to get the '49 into production as quickly as possible. Among them were new pistons, a three-blade cooling fan, larger defroster vents, water-resistant brake drums, higher-capacity heater, and significantly, more sound-deadening material. The slab-sided '49 styling was unchanged apart from a Ford crest instead of block letters on the hood. The ladder-type chassis was also untouched, continuing Ford's first-ever independent front suspension (via wishbones and coil springs), along with Hotchkiss drive and a live rear axle with hypoid differential located by longitudinal leaf springs. Also returning was the familiar engine twosome of 226-cubic-inch ohv six, rated at 95 horsepower, and venerable 239.4-cid flathead V-8 at the usual 100

bhp. Below the Crestliner was a carry-over model group comprising six-cylinder DeLuxe coupe and sedans and Custom V-8 coupe, sedans, convertible, and two-door woody wagon.

The significant 1949 design saw more extensive revisions for 1951, its final year. All models had a new face, courtesy of a thick horizontal grille bar with two small outboard bullets, and a handsomely reworked, asymmetrical dash. Except for the belated arrival of two-speed Ford-O-Matic, the company's new automatic transmission, there were no mechanical changes of note. However, the classy Crestliner was joined by a genuine pillarless hardtop, the dashing Custom V-8 Victoria. The ''Belle of the Boulevard,'' as the brochures called it, scored 110,286 sales and handily beat both Chevy's Bel Air and Plymouth's new Cranbrook Belvedere in the first battle of the low-priced hardtops. But it also

rendered the Crestliner redundant, so that model was dropped after only 8703 unit sales.

Today the Crestliner is prized by collectors for its rarity and unusual looks combined with the usual Ford virtues. It remains one ''special edition'' that truly was special.

Though outwardly little changed, the 1950 Fords boasted a number of detail revisions, most aimed at greater refinement. As the year's new top-of-the-line offering, the Crestliner was set apart from the regular Custom Tudor on which it was based by elliptical chrome bodyside moldings that delineated a contrast color panel, plus matching vinyl roof covering and standard rear fender skirts. Dash looks overly simple now, but was quite spiffy for a postwar Ford. Time-honored flathead V-8 continued at its familiar 100-bhp rating (owner: William Fink).

FORD FAIRLANE
CROWN VICTORIA 1955

While the '55 Chevy still commands a vast following, the '55 Ford garners far less attention. That's curious, because in many ways Ford was more than a match for Chevy that year. Though admittedly not "ground up" fresh, it offered colorful new styling and the most powerful engines in Ford history. And it was a solid hit, helping Ford to unprecedented model year production of over 1.4 million units—less than Chevy's but impressive all the same. Of course, high volume alone doesn't

make a great car of the Fifties or any other era, but it does reflect just how much the '55 Ford had going for it.

Basically, what Ford had going for '55 was a thoroughly reworked rendition of its successful 1952-54 platform, so heavily revised, in fact, that it almost qualified as all-new. Designer Frank Hershey modified the existing bodyshell to impart a rakish new look of motion. Highlights were a trendy wraparound windshield, full-width concave grille, deeply hooded headlamps, artfully angled "speedlines" in

the sheetmetal around the wheel openings, and modestly finned rear fenders. The lineup was now divided into four series, with wagons as a separate group and Mainline and Customline sedans as before. Replacing Crestline at the top of the heap was the new Fairlane (named after the Ford family estate in Dearborn), identified by bold chrome moldings that started above the headlamps and dipped saucily at the A-posts to end at mid-rear fender.

Besides two sedans, a Sunliner con-

vertible, and Victoria hardtop coupe, the Fairlane line included the new Crown Victoria, a hardtop-styled two-door sedan that harked back to the 1950-51 Crestliner. The work of Hershey protégé L. David Ash, it featured a novel roof with a wide chrome band raked forward from bottom to top to conceal the B-posts and wrapped up onto the roof and down the other side. Though the band looked like a rollover bar, it didn't act like one, and chief company engineer Harold T. Youngren thought enough of the body flex to specify the convertible's stiffer X-member frame. As a result, the "Crown Vicky" ended up tight and solid-feeling. Optional at $70 was a ¼-inch-thick Plexiglas roof panel, which allowed front seat occupants to look above through a bilious green tint as on the 1954 Skyliner hardtop. Only 1999 buyers exercised the op-

tion, however. The steel-top Crown Victoria saw 33,165 copies.

Ford bested Chevy in the 1955 "horsepower race" with a pair of larger engines derived from its new-for-'54 Y-block design. The basic 272-cubic-inch unit offered 162 bhp with two-barrel carb or 182 with four-barrel and dual exhausts. A 292

Though it looked like a pillarless hardtop, the 1955 Ford Crown Victoria was actually a high-style two-door sedan. Virtually all were two-toned like this pristine example, one of only 1999 built with the extra-cost Plexiglas section ahead of the "crown" roof band (owner: Chet Pollock).

previously reserved for Mercury delivered 198 bhp, and a 205-bhp "Interceptor" police special was offered on a limited basis late in the year. At the other end of the spectrum, the 223-cid Ford six was rated at 120 bhp, up five from '54.

Though the Crown Victoria was the most distinctive '55 Ford, it wouldn't last. Except for more horsepower and newly optional "Lifeguard" safety features, the '56 line saw only detail changes and lower volume. The Crown Victoria fell most of all. Just 9811 were called for. Only 603 had the "bubbletop."

Today, the distinctively styled Crown Victoria has become the focus for most '55 Ford fandom, and there aren't nearly enough to go around. So if you want one in your garage, don't pass up the next one you see for sale. As the proverb reminds us, opportunity only knocks once.

Above left: All 1955 Fords featured a new dash with "Astra Dial" instrumentation in a raised pod ahead of the driver. Three circles in the dash center housed heater/defroster controls and the radio and clock when ordered. Above: A forerunner of today's moonroof, the Crown Victoria's optional Plexiglas front roof section was a holdover from the 1954 Crestline Skyliner. Excess interior heat was the main reason for the idea's poor buyer reception. Below: All '55 Fords sported new sheetmetal over a modified 1952-54 structure. V-shaped side trim marked Fairlanes (owner: Chet Pollock).

FORD
THUNDERBIRD 1956

Americans "discovered" European sports cars in the early postwar years. Though the demand for low-slung two-seaters was always small, it was consistent enough by the early Fifties to encourage several U.S. producers to issue one of their own. Thus there appeared the Nash-Healey for 1951, the Chevrolet Corvette for 1953, and the Kaiser-Darrin for 1954.

Meanwhile, Ford Motor Company was recovering smartly from its late-Forties financial crisis, and this bolstered management's confidence in being able to take on General Motors product for product. Dearborn designers had been doodling two-seaters since about 1950, but it wasn't until the Corvette arrived that the

firm decided to get serious about one. Ford Division general manager Lewis D. Crusoe, already smitten by the exotic Europeans, now gave the go-ahead to a "personal" car with sports car overtones. The result was one of the first Fifties cars recognized as an all-time great: the 1955-57 Thunderbird.

The Thunderbird was first shown in prototype form in early 1954, and entered production on September 9. Price was set at $2944, about $200 above the Corvette. About the only thing these cars had in common was two seats. Conceived as a boulevard tourer rather than a *pur sang* sports machine, it shunned snap-in side curtains for proper roll-up windows, fiberglass bodywork for conventional

steel, and a standard six for a potent V-8, the 292-cubic-inch Mercury unit derived from Ford's capable 1954 Y-block design. With 193 horsepower in stick-shift form or 198 bhp with extra-cost Ford-O-Matic, the T-Bird had plenty of zip to go with its good looks, and it soundly trounced its Chevy rival in sales, a respectable 16,155 for the model year against 674 Corvettes.

The '56 Thunderbird changed only in detail. Its most marked difference was a "continental" exterior-mount

A standard "continental" external spare was the main visual change on the Thunderbird for '56 (owner: Alan M. Wendland & Associates).

45

Below: The '56 was the only two-seat Thunderbird with a factory-fitted outside spare, added to provide more trunk space. Near right: Dished wheel and glass ventpanes marked the '56 cockpit, which was little changed from '55 (owner: Alan M. Wendland & Associates).

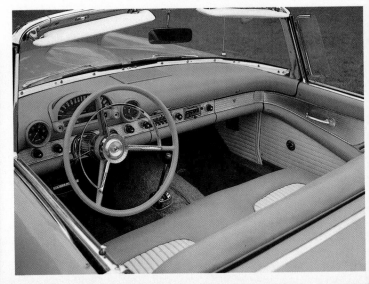

spare tire, a last-minute addition made less for styling reasons than to open up more space in the small trunk. Front fenders acquired flip-open ventilator doors to answer complaints of excessive cockpit heat, and the bolt-on accessory hardtop (a folding cloth top remained standard) could be ordered with little porthole windows, an idea from stylist Bill Boyer. The 292 V-8 was bumped to 202 bhp, and a new 312-cid engine was added, offering 215 bhp with overdrive manual or 225 bhp with automatic. List price was upped to $3151, and production leveled off slightly to 15,631 units.

With its more equal fore/aft weight distribution, the '56 was regarded as a better balanced Bird than the '55, but neither was truly sporting. The steering was slowed and the fairly stiff rear springs softened for '56 because most buyers wanted them that way, so there was more plow and less direct steering response. Yet despite its plushness, the Thunderbird proved surprisingly capable in competition. Joe Ferguson swept all honors among U.S. sports models at the 1955 Daytona Speed Weeks, averaging 124.633 mph on a two-way run to beat all foreign rivals except one Jaguar XK-120M. The next year, Ford hired Pete DePaolo to prepare a covey of Birds, and Chuck Daigh's car won the production class in the standing-mile at 88.779 mph.

For 1957, the Thunderbird was treated to a heavy face-lift, marked by a shiny bumper/grille, modest blade fins, and an extended rear deck to enclose the spare. The 292 V-8 returned along with a trio of 312s packing 245 to 285 bhp, and a small number of supercharged 312s were run off, rated at 300/340 bhp. Production was the best ever, 21,380 units, but this was because of an extra-long model year necessitated by delayed release of the all-new four-seat '58 Thunderbird.

For all the glamor it shed on the standard Ford line, the two-seat Thunderbird never sold in sufficient numbers to impress company managers. In fact, even as the first of the ''classic'' Birds came off the line, the decision had already been made to transform the model into something with much wider sales appeal. It was largely the doing of newly named Ford general manager Robert S. McNamara. But that's another story.

FORD THUNDERBIRD 1959

Perspective changes with time, and the 1958-60 Thunderbird proves it. A generation of enthusiasts once condemned the "Squarebird" as a crass business move that led to the premature demise of the classic two-seater and to the even more overblown Birds of the Sixties and Seventies.

Happily, the pioneer of personal luxury is now recognized as the great car it is. As Richard M. Langworth so astutely observed in *The Thunderbird Story*: "...all that stuff about forsaking the sports car [and] adding the hated back seat...misses the point...The 1958 Thunderbird was [perhaps] the out-

standing automotive breakthrough of the decade."

Doubts about the sales prospects for Ford's two-seat "personal" car had surfaced in December 1954, just as production was getting under way. That was enough for Robert S. McNamara, who became chief of Ford

Division early the next year. As veteran company stylist Bill Boyer recalled in *Collectible Automobile*™ magazine: "The success of that vehicle wasn't guaranteed at all...The reason they wanted to drop it was because...it wasn't a money-maker—you couldn't prove it [would yield a return] within the financial guidelines of the company." But McNamara knew a four-seater *would* make money, and he fought hard for it. Says Boyer: "[He] simply recognized that the Thunderbird image...had an immense rub-off value that you couldn't put a dollar amount on—which was unusual for Bob McNamara, because he was strictly a tightfisted financial kind of guy. The fact that he came to the defense of the Bird...astounded everybody." And he carried the day.

Reversing normal practice, Boyer's styling studio, and not Engineering, laid down the new four-seater package. Wheelbase was pegged at 113 inches (versus the two-seater's 102), and unit construction returned to Ford for the first time since the war to suit the ground-hugging stance Styling wanted. The lower 5.8-inch ground clearance left a high transmission tunnel, but it was the main stiffening member. And Boyer cleverly concealed it as a console carrying power window switches, heater/defroster controls, and a radio speaker. Further structural rigidity was provided by a massive cowl, reinforced rear deck and quarter panels, and six-inch-deep chassis siderails that created a recessed cabin floor. The all-coil suspension employed unequal-length upper and lower

Left and above: Thin-bar grille and rear lamp cluster appliqués plus chrome points on the bodyside "bombs" distinguished the '59 "Squarebird" from the '58. Top: "Gullwing" dash and pioneering center console marked 1958-60 cockpits (owner: Everett Faulkner).

A-arms up front. The rear carried a complex trailing-arm linkage intended to accommodate Ford-Aire suspension, which was scratched at the eleventh hour. The 1959-60 models reverted to ordinary leaf springs. Power was supplied by the 352-cubic-inch version of Ford's new FE-series V-8, rated at 300 horsepower. The standard transmission was a three-speed column-shift manual with available overdrive, but most buyers opted for three-speed Cruise-O-Matic automatic.

Offered as a convertible and hardtop coupe, the new T-Bird was a smash. Famed tester Tom McCahill curiously termed it a "sedan with fairly live characteristics, capable of turning 0-60 mph in 9.9 seconds." But buyers loved its sporty luxury and snapped up close to 40,000 of the '58s, nearly twice as many as the last two-seaters. McNamara had been vindicated.

Despite the new T-Bird's fairly revolutionary nature, Ford Division was allotted only $5 million for design and body/chassis/engine engineering, plus another $2 million for model changes through 1960. Cost overruns on convertible development more

than ate up the last, however, so the '59 was a virtual rerun. The main revisions were the 350-bhp Lincoln 430-cid V-8 as a new option and a late-season, fully automatic convertible top. The 1960 got triple rear lamps, a gaudier grille, more standard equipment, and a new extra-cost sliding steel sunroof, the first in U.S. postwar production. Despite the minimal mods, the "Squarebird" continued to sell like gangbusters: over 67,000 of the '59s and nearly 91,000 of the '60s. The

latter turned out to be a T-Bird record that wouldn't be surpassed until 1977.

With all this, the "Squarebird" is clearly a great car of the Fifties. The mystery is why it took us so long to recognize it.

This pristine '59 Thunderbird convertible wears the rare dealer-installed "continental kit" and tricolor wheel covers. Rear-hinged decklid completely concealed the folded top (owners: Fred Davidson & Herb Rothman).

HUDSON ITALIA 1954

Hudson vanished from the roster of makes after 1957, but it likely wouldn't have made it that far were it not for the 1954 merger with Nash that created American Motors. As an independent, the company had gone broke trying to sell six-cylinder Hornets in a V-8 market and compact Jets against 18-foot-long chrome cruisers. But had things worked out differently, Hudson would have completely restyled for 1955 and might even have introduced its own V-8, the first in its history. At the heart of these stillborn plans was the car you see here, the intriguing Italia.

Conceived by Hudson's inventive chief designer Frank Spring, the Italia was the firm's answer to the growing interest in sports cars among U.S. buyers in the early Fifties. It toured the auto show circuit in both Europe and America, presumably with the intention of perking up Hudson's flagging image as well as testing public reaction to its styling and basic concept. The show car/prototype was built around mechanicals from the lowly Jet on a 100-inch wheelbase, and carried a special dash, Alfa-Romeo steering wheel, leather upholstery, and a die-cast grille. A favorable reception encouraged Hudson to order 25 copies built on the production Jet's 105-inch-wheelbase chassis and "pro-dified" with Jet instruments and steering wheel, leather and vinyl cabin trim, and a stamped grille. Assembly and bodywork for all Italias was contracted to Carrozzeria Touring in Milan, Italy, which gave Hudson the same sort of expertise in low-volume production that Ghia was supplying to Chrysler at the time.

The Italia was displayed as "a family car with undreamed-of styling, luxury, and comfort," and Hudson hinted that it might become something more than just an interesting two-seat limited edition. In fact, it already was: the blueprint for the planned '55 restyle that wouldn't happen. Spring's design maintained recent Hudson tradition with unit construction employing a "Step-down" passenger compartment floor, as on the bulky 1948-54 models, but the styling was unlike anything the firm

A rare sight today, this is one of only 25 "production" Italias built for 1954 (owner: Kathy Crasweller).

had ever produced. Sitting nearly 10 inches lower than a standard Hudson, the jaunty coupe sported the now-obligatory wrapped windshield, plus a crisp thin-pillar roofline, gently bulging bodysides with semi-enclosed wheel openings, and a simple, Ferrari-like oval grille. The front bumper was peaked in the center to house Hudson's triangle logo, and functional scoops above the headlamps and ahead of the rear wheels ducted air to the brakes. The only jarring note was the overstyled rear end, with a vertical bank of three chromeplated tubes on each side. They looked like exhaust pipes but actually housed the tail, backup, and directional lamps. Borrani wire wheels completed the package. Most examples were finished in a light cream color. Bodies were made of aluminum in accordance with Touring's patented Superleggera (lightweight) construction.

Doors were cut 14 inches into the roof to ease entry/exit for passengers, who enjoyed ample room while sitting on unique "anatomical" seats. A first for an American producer was flow-through ventilation, via cowl air intakes and extractor slots above the nearly vertical rear window.

For all its advances, the Italia was flawed as a production prototype. For one thing, it performed no better than the Jet—no surprise, since it used the 202-cubic-inch, 114-horsepower Jet six and weighed about the same. An Italia took 15 seconds to reach 60 mph from rest and topped out at just 95 mph, versus 11 seconds and 106 mph for a '54 Corvette. Then too, the Italian-

made body was apparently very loose, and Hudson's conservative engineers held little hope for the wild styling. High price was the final blow, and Italia sales manager Roy D. Chapin, Jr. (later AMC president) had trouble shoving even 25 out the door at $4800 a copy, $1300 higher than a Corvette. "I got rid of them," he said, "[but] it wasn't one of my greatest accom-

plishments.''

Still, these were problems that might have been solved, but Hudson was on the ropes and there was simply no money. The firm did manage a prototype four-door Italia derivative on a 124-inch wheelbase, powered by the Hornet's mighty 170-bhp, 306-cid six. Called X-161, it proved prohibitively expensive for production.

Ironically, it was similar in some ways to what finally emerged, the Nash-based '55 that Hudson fans still snub as the ''Hash.''

Today, the Italia is prized by collectors as a great car of the Fifties that didn't get a chance to prove it. Too bad. With a little extra work, it might have made all the difference and Hudson would be with us yet.

While all Italias carried aluminum bodywork by Touring of Italy, the 25 ''production'' examples differed from the show car/prototype in using the instruments, the steering wheel, and the 114-bhp, 202-cid six from Hudson's compact Jet, as well as its 105-inch-wheelbase chassis. Two-seat cabin boasted ''anatomical'' seats and a fairly deep aft baggage shelf. Interior trim was leather and vinyl, versus full leather on the prototype. Front bumper and fendertop air scoops were shaped to echo Hudson's trademark triangle logo (owner: Kathy Crasweller).

HUDSON RAMBLER 1955

Rambler was the most popular and best-known of Detroit's early postwar compacts. So imagine the confusion when the 1955 models appeared in Hudson showrooms, the same cars Nash was selling except for grille and hubcap emblems. There was no mystery in this. It was simply a sign of the Nash/Hudson merger that had formed American Motors in April 1954. A more telling one was the new line of Nash-based standard Hudsons that arrived the same year.

The merger was really a Nash takeover. Rumors about it had begun circulating in late 1953 and for a good reason: Hudson was drowning in red ink. Emerging from the war as one of the weaker independents, the firm had staked its future on the radical unit-construction "Step-down" introduced for 1948. Unhappily, the design was not amenable to easy or substantial change except at great cost, and it aged rapidly. Substantially unchanged through 1953, the Step-down saw dwindling sales, aggravated by a weak dealer network, which diminished funds for developing a replacement, not to mention a V-8 engine of the sort buyers were clamoring for at the time.

But management's key miscalculation was the Jet. Launched for 1953, this ugly, underpowered compact didn't sell, but it did squander most of what money might have been spent on the Step-down's successor. Nash-Kelvinator president George Mason told Hudson chief A. E. Barit that the Jet had to go as a condition for the merger. Barit reluctantly agreed. As this left Hudson without a compact, a group of badge-engineered Ramblers was issued to substitute, the only cars dealers had to sell for the first four months or so of the 1955 model year. Interestingly, they sold nearly twice

as many Ramblers as they had 1954 Jets, a total of 25,214, plus a much smaller number of British-built Nash Metropolitan two-seaters.

Whether called Nash or Hudson, the 1955 Rambler was largely the same as the introductory 1950 model that Mason had doggedly pushed into production. An interim face-lift for 1953 brought a closer family resemblance with the big Farina-styled Nash of the previous year. For '54, the existing 100-inch-wheelbase two-door wagon, convertible, and Country Club hardtop coupe were joined by a new four-door sedan and Cross Country wagon on a 108-inch wheelbase, the longer chassis providing easier rear entry/exit. This basic lineup returned for '55, arrayed in DeLuxe, Super, and Custom models as before. Styling changes were limited to an eggcrate grille, replacing the previous floating-bar affair, and fully open front wheel cutouts instead

The Nash Rambler came to Hudson showrooms for 1955 with the appropriate badges and slightly fewer models. Shown is the 100-inch-wheelbase Custom Country Club hardtop coupe, the top of Hudson's compact line, priced at $2098 (owner: Bill Barbee).

of the former semi-enclosed type that had made the turning circle much too wide for such a small car. Unit construction was retained per Nash tradition, along with the sturdy but old L-head six (it dated from 1941) in the 195.6-cubic-inch size adopted for 1953. Nash offered more Rambler models at prices that bracketed the Hudson spectrum, which ran from $1457 for the DeLuxe business sedan to $2098 for the Custom Country Club hardtop.

For 1956, AMC standardized the 108-inch chassis for a totally new Rambler with much jazzier styling. Again there were identical Nash and Hudson versions, but this minor distinction vanished for 1957. The marques vanished the next year, when the 100-inch-wheelbase Rambler made a surprise return as the American. Remarkably, it survived all the way through model year 1963.

Longevity and significance as the pioneer postwar compact earn the early-Fifties Ramblers their status as ''great cars'' today. Moreover, you just don't see many of the Hudsons anymore, and that counts for something among car fans.

Fully open front wheel cutouts and a new eggcrate grille marked all '55 Ramblers, which were otherwise little changed from 1952-54 (owner: Bill Barbee).

KAISER 1951

Landmark styling is the main reason the second-generation Kaiser stands as a great car of the Fifties. The 1951 model and its 1952-55 descendants represented a design peak for the U.S. industry, and they still look good now: rakish, clean, beautifully balanced. Yet it was this same advanced styling that led to Kaiser-Frazer's ultimate demise—that and inept management.

America's independent carmakers were never more successful than in the late Forties, and none made a bigger splash than Kaiser-Frazer. Uniting west coast construction and shipbuilding tycoon Henry J. Kaiser with 35-year auto industry veteran Joseph Frazer, the "postwar wonder company" confounded skeptics by launching production in June 1946 after converting the mile-and-a-half-long bomber factory at Willow Run, Michigan into the world's largest car plant under one roof. By New Year's Day 1950, K-F had built some 400,000 cars under the Kaiser and Frazer marques to become the industry's leading independent.

Then K-F started running into trouble. Henry had risked millions to maintain existing volume levels for 1949, the year of the Big Three's first new postwar models. But K-F had only warmed-over versions of its basic 1947-48 design, the beetle-browed four-door conceived by Howard A. "Dutch" Darrin. Henry took a bath.

Next he borrowed some $12 million to produce a compact before the market was really ready for one. Unabashedly named Henry J, it went nowhere. A third blunder was phasing out the higher-priced Frazer cars even as dealers begged for more. By the end of 1951, output at Willow Run was down 80 percent from 1948.

But all these mistakes could have been permanently erased by the "Anatomic Design" Kaiser. And for a time, they were. Introduced in

Wide lower bodyside moldings distinguished Kaiser's upper-level 1951 Deluxe models. Foglamps and windshield sunvisor were accessories (owner: Arthur J. Sabin).

February 1950, a good six months ahead of most competitors, the all-new '51 was a sensation. K-F sold 146,911 of them for the balance of 1950 to record the second-best calendar year tally of its brief history.

The '51 Kaiser was unlike any other American car of its day. Riding a 118.5-inch wheelbase, it bore fresh new styling enlarged by Duncan McRae from an original Darrin concept for a 105-inch-wheelbase compact. Highlights included a unique "sweetheart dip" in the upper rear window and windshield frames, 700 square inches more glass than its nearest rival, and the lowest beltline of any Detroit car built through 1956. Production engineering, by chief engineer Ralph Isbrandt and body specialist John Widman, involved a very rigid separate body atop an equally strong X-member frame weighing just 200 pounds. An ultra-low center of gravity plus a long-travel suspension with canted shocks made for the industry's nimblest handling, yet curb weight was only about 3100 pounds. The safety-styled interior boasted a slope-away padded dash with recessed instruments and a windshield that popped out harmlessly on impacts of more than 35 pounds per square inch. K-F's inventive color engineer, Carleton Spencer, wrapped it all up in exciting and sometimes exotic exterior hues and interior materials.

Yet the second-generation Kaiser was doomed, as was K-F itself. Sales began tapering off in 1951, due as much to high prices as to renewed Big Three competition. More telling was K-F's inability to field a V-8 engine or sportier body styles like a convertible or hardtop coupe. All were precluded by lack of tooling funds, much of which had been diverted to the abortive Henry J. Thus, K-F was stuck with only two- and four-door sedans and a lackluster 226-cubic-inch flathead six that demanded more than the usual amount of maintenance. Profits continued to fall despite a 1952 face-lift, price and equipment juggling for 1953, and a very effective makeover plus optional supercharged power for '54. An ill-advised 1953 merger with Willys provided no relief. After completing just 270 of its 1955 models, Kaiser called it quits in the United States.

Ironically, the second generation lived on in Argentina as the 1958-62 Kaiser Carabela. It lives on today as a breakthrough design that deserved a better fate.

The second-generation Kaiser boasted roomy, "safety-styled" interiors with padded dash, neatly clustered instruments, and terrific outward visibility. Dutch Darrin's original design survived into production with a raised rear roof the only major change. Lower back seat improved headroom on the 1952-55 models. This fully restored '51 Deluxe four-door was discovered with only some 11,500 actual miles and is a national K-F O   rs Club meet winner (owner: Arthur J. Sabin).

MERCURY 1951

Enthusiasts enshrined the 1949-51 Mercury long ago, not for its abilities as a production car but for its possibilities as a custom car. In the Fifties, ''bathtub'' Mercs modified with chopped tops, cruiser skirts, borrowed taillamps and grilles, and lowered, highly decorated bodies were a common sight at high schools everywhere. Perhaps there was something about the styling that invited such treatment: clean, rounded, massive. There's no doubt that movie idol James Dean seared the custom Merc into the collective consciousness

of a generation by driving one in *Rebel Without a Cause*. Whatever the reason, no Mercury had so fired the imagination of America's youth—and it would be a long time before one would again.

The 1949-51 Mercury was something of a fluke. Ford Motor Company's initial postwar model planning envisioned two separate Mercury lines on wheelbases of 120 and 123 inches. Below these were two Fords: a 100-inch-wheelbase ''Light Car'' compact and a standard-size model group on a 118-inch chassis. Rounding

out the corporate lineup was a trio of Lincolns: a 125-inch-wheelbase standard offering, a Cosmopolitan/Custom series on a three-inch longer span, and a new Continental and limousine on a 132-inch wheelbase.

Ultimately, these plans were sidetracked by Ernest R. Breech, recruited in 1945 by newly named

The 1951 Mercury convertible carried a $2370 base price. Small emblems below the fuel filler flap identify newly optional Merc-O-Matic (owner: Bob Ward).

Top and center: A bolder grille and squared-up rear fenders marked all '51 Mercurys, including the coupe, which vied with the convertible as the customizers' favorite (owner: Dan Adams). Above: The clean tail of the '51 Sport Sedan (owner: James Adams).

company president Henry Ford II to be his second-in-command. Breech thought the proposed Ford was too heavy and ponderous. Moreover, marketing studies suggested the compact was premature in the booming postwar seller's market, and a Continental continuation seemed like a questionable use of scarce funds in view of the model's limited sales potential. In August 1946, Breech recommended to Ford's policy committee that the two Mercury lines be combined into one lower-priced Lincoln series, that a single Mercury line be fielded based on the proposed Ford, and that a new Ford on a 114-inch chassis be developed with all due speed. Naturally, the committee endorsed all his "suggestions."

As a result, the first new postwar Mercury appeared for 1949 on a 118-inch wheelbase, sharing basic body structure with the three-inch longer standard Lincoln (the upper-level Cosmo rode a 125-inch chassis). Styling, finalized during the war by chief company designer E. T. Bob Gregorie, embodied "second-generation" streamlining concepts, and it was right in step with the times. Under the hood was a stroked version of the Ford/Mercury flathead V-8 venerated by hot rodders, now at 255.4 cubic inches and 110 horsepower—up 16 cid and 10 bhp from 1946-48. The single series comprised just four body styles: two-door coupe, woody wagon, and convertible, plus a four-door Sport Sedan with throwback "suicide" rear-hinged back doors.

Mercury set a new production record for 1949, a total of 301,319. The close styling relationship with the costlier Lincolns and genuine 100-mph performance, a first for the make, were the main reasons. The 1950 edition saw only minor trim changes and slightly lower volume. Squared-up rear fenders and a busier grille appeared for '51, along with a nominal two-bhp gain in engine output and newly optional Merc-O-Matic two-speed automatic transmission. Mercury rose from sixth to ninth in industry production that year by setting another record, 310,387 units.

Custom cars are enjoying a revival today, so the "bathtub" Mercs are too. Thank goodness that some of the survivors have been left in "stock" condition for us to remember as great cars of the Fifties.

OLDSMOBILE 88 1950

The original Oldsmobile 88 is perhaps best thought of as America's first mass-production "factory hot rod." Appearing in 1949, it was an immediate hit that duly sounded the gun for the "horsepower race" of the Fifties. Moreover, it compiled an enviable competition record that firmly established Olds with a high-performance image, which would prove a key factor in the make's consistently high sales for most of the decade. With all this, the early 88 deserves a place in the automotive hall of fame.

Like most bright ideas, the 88 concept was disarmingly simple. Olds shared honors with sister division Cadillac by introducing the industry's first high-compression overhead-valve V-8 for 1949. Originally, the new 303.7-cubic-inch Olds "Rocket" engine was intended only for the senior 98 series, which—again with Cadillac—had received General Motors' first new postwar styling the previous year. With the new look being extended to the company's junior models for 1949, Olds general manager Sherrod Skinner had the brilliant notion of slotting the

compact, 135-horsepower V-8 into the lighter, Chevy-size Series 76 that was trundling around with a 105-bhp six. Voila! Instant excitement.

The result was a revelation for buyers accustomed to plodding L-head sixes and big, slow-revving straight eights. Weighing 300-500 pounds less than a 98, the typical 88 had a power-to-weight ratio of about 22.5:1, not so

DeLuxe Holiday hardtop was a new entry in the "Futuramic 88" lineup for 1950 (owner: R. G. Brelsford).

hot by standards of later years but sufficient to make this one of the quickest cars you could find on any showroom floor at the time. And with prices as low as $2143 for the standard-trim fastback club coupe, the 88 offered more go for the dough than anything else on the road. The new Rocket V-8 was a gem, with an impressive 240 lbs/ft torque, a sturdy five-main-bearing crankshaft, oversquare bore/stroke dimensions (3.75 × 3.44 inches), and tremendous internal strength. Though it ran initially on mild 7.5:1 compression, it was designed to accept ratios as high as 12:1, amazing for an everyday Detroit engine.

Oldsmobile's new hot one was an obvious stock-car racer, and it scored early, taking six of nine NASCAR Grand National events in '49 and car-

rying Red Byron to the driver's championship. The following year, an 88 broke its class record at Daytona with a two-way average of 100.28 mph, and won the first Mexican Road Race, besting formidable rivals like Alfa-Romeo, Cadillac, and Lincoln. On the ovals the 88s took 10 out of 19 contests in 1950 and 20 out of 41 in 1951. Though displaced by the Hudson Hornet as the car to beat in 1952-54, the 88 continued to show its ability—and stamina. A 1950 model nicknamed "Roarin' Relic" was still winning the occasional modified-class race as late as 1959!

Such goings-on naturally helped keep Olds sales high after the seller's market waned around 1950. The division sold about 397,000 cars that year. It didn't do as well in 1951-53, but it

never fell below eighth place in production.

Model year 1950 brought minor styling changes and a "Futuramic 88" lineup expanded with Harley Earl's pillarless hardtop coupe body style, offered as the standard and DeLuxe Holiday. The 88 was supplanted as the hot ticket for '51 by the new Super 88, basically a restyled version of the same popular idea.

There would be a lot of fast Oldsmobiles to come in the Fifties, but the 88 was the first. Today, it's revered as the granddaddy of Detroit muscle.

The fastback club coupe body style put in its last appearance at Oldsmobile for 1950. Shown is the hot "Futuramic 88" version in DeLuxe trim (owner: Philip Arneson).

OLDSMOBILE 98 1959

Oldsmobile won 1959's Most Improved Styling Award hands down. It wasn't difficult. Almost anything would have been an improvement on the chrome-covered '58s, and the new design definitely was: dramatically '59 and much cleaner. Proclaimed as "The Linear Look," it earned bouquets instead of brickbats from critics and customers alike.

That ad slogan was apt. The '59 not only looked longer, lower, and wider, it was. Despite only fractional gains in wheelbase, overall length went up by more than 10 inches on the low-line Dynamic 88 and mid-pack Super 88 and by six inches on the posh 98 series. Bodies bulged outward to accommodate front and rear tracks widened by two and three inches, respectively (now 61 inches each), and overall height came down by 1.5 inches, which lowered the center of gravity for slightly better handling. Olds stylists accentuated the new dimensions with a mile-wide grille dominated by broadly spaced horizontal quad headlamps, plus a flat, expansive hood and sculptured rear quarters that suggested fins in a straight-through fenderline. General Motors' new corporate body-sharing program gave the 98 its own shell for the first time since 1951, but all models boasted massive, compound-curve windshields. Four-door hardtops, now called Holiday Sport-Sedans, emphasized "The Linear Look" with a flat roofline extending just beyond a radically wrapped rear window. On two-door hardtops, now called SceniCoupes, the greenhouse

Priced at $4366, the 98 convertible was the costliest '59 Olds. Like other 98s, it rode a new 126.3-inch wheelbase and measured a sizable 223 inches long overall. All models featured concave back panels with built-in trunk handles. Color-coded "Safety Spectrum" speedometer was new this year (owner: Ralph R. Leid).

was shorter and the backlight taller, arched into the roof like the windshield.

Supporting these impressively sized structures was a brand-new chassis with perimeter siderails and a long X-member with a short tunnel in its center. A large rectangular section aft of the rear axle carried the rear of the body, which was unitized from the firewall back. Rear leaf springs for the solid axle and front coils with twin A-arm geometry continued to support the wheels. Air suspension was still available but found very few takers.

Olds continued to rely on its proven and potent Rocket V-8 for '59, with the same basic block introduced a decade before. The lighter 88s used the 371.1-cubic-inch enlargement introduced for '57, with 270 horsepower in standard tune or 300 optional. New was a bigger-bore 394-cid unit for the Super 88 and 98, rated at 315 bhp. Compression was 9.75:1 across the board. Though manual transmission was still nominally offered, optional self-shift Hydra-Matic remained the overwhelming buyer preference.

Priced at $4366, the 98 convertible repeated at the top of an Olds lineup comprising 15 models for '59. Power vent windows were the year's only new optional gadget, but six-way power seats, padded dash, air conditioning, improved ''Roto-Matic'' power steering, and a redesigned take-along ''Trans-portable'' AM radio could all be ordered. The showroom-new beauty you see here carries rear fender skirts, an item not usually specified by Oldsmobile's typically conservative clientele.

Olds had a mixed year in '59. Despite slightly higher production of close to 383,000 units, the division fell from fourth to sixth in the model year rankings. Oddly, Olds had moved from fifth to fourth for '58, so maybe the brightwork brigade was on to something after all.

Yet the '59 was a timely and tasteful turnaround that set the stage for Olds elegance in the Sixties. Enough said.

Left: New 394-cid V-8 offered 315 bhp in the '59 Olds 98. Below: Back panel lettering is tricky to read (owner: Ralph R. Leid).

PACKARD FOUR HUNDRED 1955

Packard perished for the reason most companies do: mismanagement. But before its ultimate tragedy came technological triumph in the memorable 1955-56 models. They wouldn't be the last to bear the name, but they would be the last "real" Packards.

Troubles had been mounting for Packard ever since World War II. Most were of its own making. Stodgy styling, continued reliance on straight eights in a V-8 market, and the more limited resources of an independent company all contributed to a sales decline that accelerated in the early Fifties. But the main problem was

Packard's stubborn refusal to abandon the medium-price field it had embraced for survival in the Depression. Most analysts agree that in 1945, when Detroit could sell almost anything, Packard should have returned to the luxury class exclusively. It didn't, and the price was high. After moving over 100,000 cars in 1949 at the height of the postwar seller's market, Packard saw sales sag by 25 percent in 1950-51. The next year, the total dropped by half.

Hopes for recovery brightened in May 1952 when the energetic James J. Nance swept in to replace aging Hugh Ferry as company president. Nance quickly scheduled a complete restyle

and the firm's first-ever V-8 for 1954, but Packard's ill-advised acquisition of Studebaker that year delayed both these badly needed, long-overdue developments until 1955. It's just as well, because rival Chrysler bought Packard's chief body supplier, Briggs Manufacturing Company, in 1954. Curiously, Nance set up the '55 body line in a cramped plant on Detroit's Conner Avenue rather than at Packard's older but roomier main facility on East Grand Boulevard. The results were

The 1955 Packard Four Hundred hardtop coupe cost $3930 new. Production was 7206 units (owner: Harold Gibson).

69

constant production tie-ups and major quality control problems.

Despite these woes, the 1955 Packard was a marvel. Leading its features list was "Torsion-Level" suspension, with the front and rear wheels on each side linked by long longitudinal torsion bars, bolstered by a complicated electric self-leveler that automatically adjusted for changes in weight distribution. Torsion-Level endowed the senior Packards with extraordinary ride and handling, no mean feat considering their 127-inch wheelbases and curb weights of over two tons. Nance's new V-8 provided extraordinary performance, emerging as a conventional short-stroke design with

typical Packard strength and reliability. At 352 cubic inches it delivered 260 horsepower in the big Patrician sedan/ Four Hundred hardtop, a rousing 275 bhp with four-barrel carburetor in the limited-edition Caribbean convertible. Last but not least was Richard A. Teague's masterful makeover of John Reinhart's dated 1951-54 "high pockets" bodyshell. Its main elements were peaked front fenders, massive eggcrate grille, modestly wrapped windshield, jazzy side trim, and distinctive "cathedral" taillamps.

The '55 Packard was a stunning achievement for a company that was, by that time, deep in financial hot water. Despite the patchwork and

trouble-prone new "Twin-Ultramatic" transmission, Packard-Clipper Division recorded a small profit by producing nearly 70,000 cars for calendar 1955, triple the previous year's total. But this was more than offset by Studebaker's staggering losses, and quality control bugs persisted on the mildly changed '56s. Packard's past had now caught up with its present. After a token appearance on restyled Studebakers for 1957-58, this once-proud marque was mercifully put to rest.

The last real Packards are a fitting tribute to Jim Nance who, sadly, passed away in 1984. No one ever gave more to save a car company. What a pity the odds were against him.

Stylist Richard A. Teague worked miracles in giving Packard's aging 1951-54 body a fresh look for '55. Wrapped windshield, massive egg-crate grille, and handsome ''cathedral'' taillights identified this year's senior models like this Four Hundred hardtop. Glittery ''Reynolds Wrap'' bodyside trim was another feature. Teague also conceived a ''circle-V'' logo as a new/old timeless symbol for Packard, but it didn't last long (owner: Harold Gibson).

PLYMOUTH FURY 1957

Buyers must have had a tough time choosing among the "Low-Price Three" for 1957. It was a vintage year for the U.S. auto industry in general and this trio in particular. A heavily revamped Chevrolet appealed for its new "junior Cadillac" look and extra go from a larger V-8 with optional fuel injecton. This year's Ford was all-new, boasting "Thunderbird" power

in a bigger package plus a jazzier, more youthful appearance. But only Plymouth could claim styling that was "3 Full Years Ahead," plus the most available horsepower and the best handling in its field. It made a lot of shoppers think twice.

Not surprisingly, many of them chose Plymouth—more than ever, in fact. Chrysler Corporation's perennial

breadwinner had scored a numerical triumph with record production in calendar 1955. Now it added a moral victory by regaining its customary third place in the model year volume stakes for the first time since 1954,

The low-volume Fury returned from '56 as the priciest '57 Plymouth. It sold new for $2925 (owner: Richard Carpenter).

Plymouth's all-new '57 styling was promoted heavily in "Suddenly It's 1960!" ads. Gold-tint grille and side trim made the top-line Fury easy to spot (owner: Richard Carpenter).

with a smashing 762,231 units, up more than 200,000 from '56. In what was generally conceded at the time as Chrysler's year, Plymouth was the biggest success by far.

It's not hard to understand why: from road to roof, the '57 was a revolution, especially for a low-price make. Its styling embodied the best ideas of Chrysler design chief Virgil Exner, with the same pleasing balance, overall purity of line, and crisp surface development that marked the

firm's other products this year. Like them, Plymouth bore a new dart-shaped profile, with greatly increased glass area and a much lower beltline. Setting it apart were prominent "shark" fins, forward-thrusting front fenders, and a cross-hatch grille riding above a raised central stone shield. The '57s not only looked longer and lower, they were. Overall height came down three inches on sedans and five inches on hardtops, and wheelbase stretched by three inches (to 118) on all body styles except wagons, where it grew by seven (to 122 inches). It all added up to the slickest Plymouth in history, and "buff book" writers went scurrying for superlatives. Dell Publishing's editors named it "Style

Car of the Year." Said *Popular Mechanics:* "The 1957 styling is spectacular in a very refined way. There's nothing gaudy about it. In fact, it has the quiet, fashionable look of a dream car."

The '57 Plymouth certainly drove like a dream. There was a completely new frame with two extra crossmembers (five in all) for greater rigidity, plus Chrysler's stellar new torsion-bar front suspension for flatter, nimbler handling. Semi-elliptic leaf springs were retained at the rear, but were rerated and moved further outboard, which also enhanced roll control. Despite all this, ride was actually improved.

So was performance. Power was up across the board, beginning with the humble 230.2-cubic-inch "Powerflow" six that was standard for all models except the Belvedere convertible and the limited-edition Fury hardtop. The 277-cid "HyFire" V-8 returned with 197 bhp, up 10 bhp from '56, and there was new 301-cid Fury V-8 with 8.5:1 compression and 215 bhp in standard form or 235 bhp with extra-cost "PowerPak" four-barrel carburetor. Oddly, the last wasn't available on the Fury itself. But that was okay, because the hottest Plymouth now carried a standard 318-cid V-8 packing 290 bhp with 9.25:1 compression and twin quad carburetors. Called the Fury V-800, this most potent version of Chrysler's polyspherical-head design was made an option for any Plymouth later in the season. Sensibly, it was packaged with uprated chassis components.

Introduced for '56, the hardtop Fury was simply sensational in '57 form. As before, it was set apart from lesser models by gold-anodized inserts for the normal Belvedere body-side sweepspears and came only in monotone white (actually cream). The '57 arrived in January of that year, about two months behind the rest of the line, and was priced at $2925, which made it the priciest Plymouth by far. Production totaled only 7438 units.

Somewhere along the way to the '57 redesign, Chrysler Corporation workmanship slipped badly and its cars lost the relative corrosion resistance they'd had through 1956. This makes any 1957 Plymouth, and the Fury in particular, a rare commodity today, but one worth seeking. Great go and great styling add up to a great car of the Fifties not to be missed.

PONTIAC BONNEVILLE 1957

History sometimes repeats itself by working in reverse. Take Pontiac's once-familiar "Silver Streaks." Division general manager William S. Knudsen had put them on the hoods of his 1935 models to spiff up their styling and thus improve sales. They remained a Pontiac fixture until his son yanked them off 20 years later—for the same reason! "We had to get rid of that 'Indian concept,'" said Semon E. "Bunkie" Knudsen in 1978. "No reflection on the American Indian, but old Chief Pontiac had been associated in the public mind with a prosaic, family-toting sedan from the time Pontiacs were first built."

Pontiac's image definitely needed rejuvenating when Bunkie took on his father's old job in mid-1956, and he hustled. There had already been timely shots in the sales arm with fresh new styling and the division's first ohv V-8 for 1955, followed by more displacement and horsepower for '56. Though Bunkie could do little else about styling for the '57s, he could give the make another infusion of youthfulness by stepping up performance—and Pontiac's presence on the racing warpath. He quickly hired Elliott M. "Pete" Estes as chief engineer and put him to work on extra carburetors and higher compression. One of the first results appeared at mid-model year as the legendary Tri-Power setup, with a trio of two-barrel carbs on a special manifold atop a newly

enlarged 347-cubic-inch version of Pontiac's versatile 1955 V-8. Next, Bunkie hired famed Daytona Beach mechanic Smokey Yunick to prepare it for the track, and the Knudsen-sponsored car ran a record 131.747-mph lap at that year's Speed Weeks. When the Automobile Manufacturers Association issued its infamous racing "ban" in early '57, Knudsen took Pontiac underground, retaining Yunick for development work and later resuming ties with tuner Ray Nichels.

Pontiac's bold Bonneville appeared in February 1957. Fuel-injected 370 V-8 was standard (owner: Joseph E. Bortz).

Bunkie had something else up his sleeve: a hot limited edition designed to bring throngs of performance-seekers into Pontiac showrooms. It bowed in February 1957 with a perfect name: Bonneville. Knudsen later described it as "the car I was counting on to bring the new message to the public. And it did. I remember sitting in the grandstand at Daytona...at its first race. Somebody...shouted, 'Look what's happened to Grandma!'" The reason: "Grandma" had been to Vic Tanny.

Announced at $5782 and "for dealer use only," the Bonneville was the most muscular Pontiac yet. It was offered only as a convertible on the top-line Star Chief series' 124-inch wheelbase. Standard equipment included Strato-Flight Hydra-Matic, power steering and brakes, unique "spinner" wheel covers, and numerous accessories that cost extra on lesser models. Distinguishing styling features were anodized-aluminum gravel shields on the lower rear

fenders, "hash mark" front fender trim, and a chrome-plated bullet set within the spear-like bodyside moldings adopted as part of this year's restyle. The result was a car that looked longer and lower than its linemates despite the three-year-old, Chevy-shared bodyshell.

But the Bonneville's main attraction was advertised by bold front fender nameplates that read "Fuel Injection." Under the hood was a bored-out 370-cid V-8 rated at 300-plus horsepower, courtesy of the new Rochester system designed by GM Engineering and shepherded into production by Harry Barr and Corvette wizard Zora Arkus-Duntov. It was similar to the Ramjet system introduced that same year by Chevrolet (the only other domestic make to offer fuel injection on a production model), but it was a tidier setup allegedly designed for maximum low-range torque rather than top-end power. It consisted of separate fuel and air meters on a special manifold assembly that sat

where the carburetor and intake manifold normally would. Fuel was injected directly into each port, making this what we now call a "multipoint" system.

For all that, the Bonneville actually proved slower in all-out acceleration than the Tri-Power Pontiacs, particularly the lighter Chieftains. *Motor Trend* timed one at a consistent 18 seconds in the standing quarter-mile— fast but not breathtaking—and obtained decent fuel economy of 17-18 miles per gallon. But none of this really mattered. Though only 630 of the '57s were built, the Bonneville was just the sort of tonic "Grandma" needed for the sales race. For 1958, it became a separate series with a hardtop coupe as well as a convertible, and over 12,000 were sold. The rest is history.

"You can sell an old man a young man's car," Bunkie once said, "but you can never sell a young man an old man's car." Starting with the '57 Bonneville, Pontiac wouldn't be caught doing that again.

Like Chevy's, the 1955-56 Pontiac bodyshell was given a heavy face-lift for '57, its final year. Longer rear deck and fenders and a shinier front dressed it up. Chrome-plated bodyside ''bombs'' and ''spinner'' wheel covers made Bonneville the brashest of the bunch. Dash was redone too, but its shiny surfaces would never pass muster in the safety-conscious Eighties (owner: Joesph E. Bortz).

STUDEBAKER
HAWK 1957

Studebaker stole the styling spotlight for 1953 with a pair of racy-looking, low-slung two-doors, the pillared Starlight coupe and pillarless Starliner hardtop. Created under the aegis of famed designer Raymond Loewy, they were an eye-opening achievement for an American automaker and quickly earned critical acclaim at home and abroad. South Bend might have sold many more than it did had management not biased production in favor of the much dumpier sedans and wagons derived from this basic design. By the time things got sorted out, buyers were looking elsewhere, and adding more tinsel didn't do much for sales over

the succeeding two years. Studebaker seemed headed for oblivion.

But the '53 tooling still had a lot of life in it, so the firm gamely restyled for 1956. Appearing alongside a more upright, squared-off group of standard Studebakers was what ads trumpeted as "the first full line of family sports cars." It went by the name of Hawk.

The 1956 Hawk would be Loewy's last effort for Studebaker until the Avanti of six years later, and it was striking: busier than the '53 original but much cleaner and more "European" than the gaudy '55. Studebaker-

Packard president James J. Nance insisted on a full line of cars in all price ranges, so there were no fewer than four Hawks. At the bottom of the

Wilder concave metal fins marked the '57 Golden Hawk, which handled much better than its '56 predecessor thanks to adoption of a lighter, supercharged Studebaker 289 V-8 in place of the heavy 352 Packard engine (owner: Bob Patrick).

Above and below: A fiberglass hood overlay and revised taillamps also marked the '57 Golden Hawk, which remained an effective makeover of the original 1953-54 "Loewy coupe" design. This year's blown 289 V-8 put out the same 275 bhp as the 1956 version's Packard engine. Right: Note the unusual factory seat belts (owner: Bob Patrick).

pecking order was the $1986 Flight Hawk, powered by Stude's aging 101-horsepower, 185.6-cubic-inch L-head six. Next was the Power Hawk, with the same attractive styling and tighter pillared body but powered by the familiar 259.2-cid, 170-bhp Commander V-8 and priced at just over $2100. Then came the Sky Hawk, with pillarless construction, this year's new 210-bhp 289-cid V-8, and a price tag just shy of $2500. Topping the line was the $3061 Golden Hawk, packing the big—and heavy—352-cid Packard engine with 275 bhp and marked by little fiberglass fins tacked on over the rear fender seams.

At less than 20,000 unit sales, the '56 Hawk did little to stem the tide of red ink in South Bend. The line was duly trimmed to two models for 1957: a revised Golden Hawk and a pillared Silver Hawk. New chief stylist Duncan McRae added larger, concave metal fins to both and eliminated the old bodyside contour lines. The Golden Hawk now carried a supercharged version of the Studebaker 289, which took 100 ponderous pounds off its front end and made a world of difference in its handling. The Silver Hawk had the old six as standard, but the unblown 289 in 210- and 225-bhp form was optional. A late-season arrival was the "ultra-smart" Golden Hawk 400, offering hand-buffed, top-grain leather upholstery for about $500 more than the normal model. Despite all these changes, sales stayed about the same.

Production plummeted by more than half for 1958, when the little-changed Golden and Silver Hawk were joined by a badge-engineered Packard cousin with the same Studebaker mechanicals and an awful "catfish mouth" front. Fortunately, it lasted only a year. Sales continued in the cellar for '59, when Studebaker pinned its hopes on the compact Lark and fielded a lone Silver Hawk. The 1960 edition dropped the Silver designation and the six, but sales slumped badly. The Hawk's final year was 1961, with a four-speed manual gearbox the main attraction. Only 3929 of these cars were built.

The Hawk would live on with a dramatic Brooks Stevens face-lift as the Gran Turismo Hawk of 1962-64. Today, the finny Fifties models are appreciated as prophets of the Sixties sporty compact craze. How sad they were without honor in their own time.